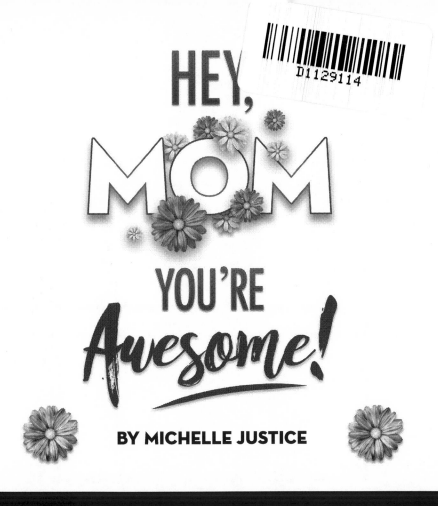

HEY, MOM YOU'RE Awesome!

BY MICHELLE JUSTICE

CREATE THE PERFECT GIFT FOR MOM BY PERSONALIZING THIS BOOK JUST FOR HER!

This **WHAT I LOVE ABOUT MOM** fill-in-the-blank book contains lines to describe why your mom's the best. There are also fun checklists, places to paste in photos (or better yet draw something fun), memes, corny puns, coloring book pages and more!

Make it funny, heartfelt or as sentimental as you want...she'll love your personal touches!

THE ULTIMATE BEST MOM IN THE WORLD GIFT!
She'll read it over and over again!

DEDICATED TO:

My always supportive mother,
Marlene.
It's impossible to thank you properly
for everything you've done.
From telling me I could do anything
I set my mind to... to dishing out
some tough love when I needed it.

Thank you mom, for helping to
become the person I am today.

I Love You!
Michelle

If you love this book...
would you please leave us a review?

ISBN: 978-1-949361-45-2

TO: The Best Mom Ever!

FROM: _____

DATE: _____

What I love about Mom?
This little book all about you answers that question.

I love that you're my mom because...

ROSES ARE RED...
VIOLETS ARE BLUE...
I'M SO LUCKY TO HAVE A...
MOM LIKE YOU!

When I was a kid, I thought the best thing about you was...

MOMS
ARE LIKE BUTTONS

THEY HOLD EVERYTHING TOGETHER

What makes you special and different from other moms is...

"DO SMALL THINGS WITH GREAT LOVE."
—MOTHER TERESA

SUPERLIST #1

Mom, here are things I **learned from you**
that I hope to teach someone else someday:

[CHECK ALL THAT APPLY]

❑ Cooking

❑ Friendliness

❑ Driving

❑ Wallpapering

❑ Painting

❑ Common Sense

❑ Tie Shoelaces

❑ Make Coffee

❑ Right from Wrong

❑ Laundry

❑ Gardening

❑ Compassion

❑ Pay Bills

❑ Dance

❑ Solving Crosswords

❑ Studying

❑ Sewing

❑ Knitting

❑ Different Language

❑ Sarcasm

❑ Joke Telling

❑ Fold a Fitted Sheet

❑ _____

"NOT A
DAISY
GOES BY THAT I DON'T THINK OF YOU."

Without you, I never would have...

MOM
IS JUST
WOW
UPSIDE DOWN.

It makes me smile when you...

"A MOTHER'S ARMS ARE MORE COMFORTING
THAN ANYONE ELSE'S."
– PRINCESS DIANA

Thank you for inspiring me to...

"IF I HAD A SINGLE FLOWER FOR EVERY TIME I THINK OF YOU...
I COULD WALK FOREVER IN MY GARDEN." – CLAUDIA GHANDI

SUPERLIST #2

Mom, if you were a **FLOWER** you would be a...

[CHECK ALL THAT APPLY]

☐ **ROSE**
Love & appreciation

☐ **GLADIOLUS**
Strength of character,
faithfulness and honor.

☐ **HYDRANGEA**
Heartfelt emotions.
Gratitude for being understood.

☐ **BIRD OF PARADISE**
Joyfulness & magnificence.

☐ **ORCHID**
Exotic beauty. Refinement,
thoughtfulness, mature
charm and glorious femininity.

☐ **SNAPDRAGON**
Graciousness and strength

☐ **PEONY**
Compassion. Happy life,
good health and prosperity.

☐ **SUNFLOWER**
Pure thoughts. Adoration
and dedication.

☐ **CHRYSANTHEMUM**
Optimism, joy & long life.

☐ **IRIS**
Eloquence. Wisdom,
compliments, faith and hope.

☐ _____

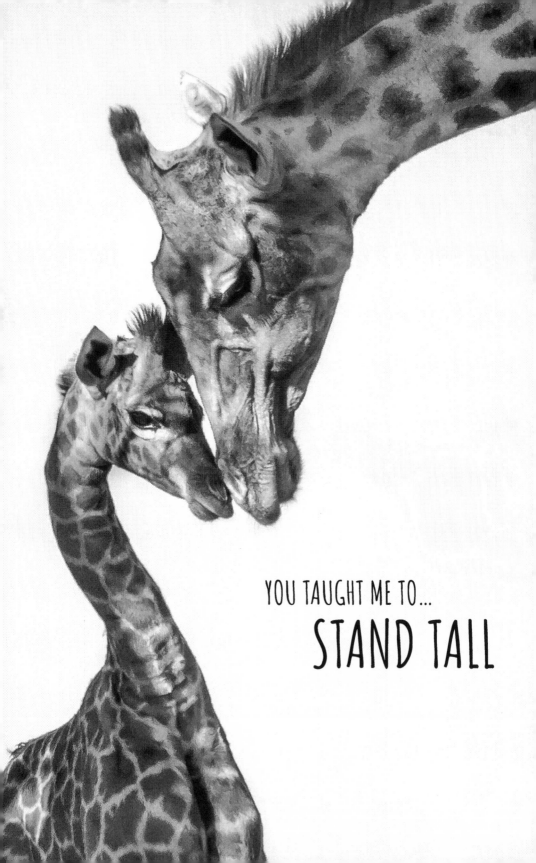

YOU TAUGHT ME TO...
STAND TALL

My clearest memory of you from childhood is...

"MOTHERHOOD:
ALL LOVE BEGINS AND ENDS THERE."
—ROBERT BROWNING

From you, I learned the importance of......

"ALL THAT I AM, OR HOPE TO BE,
I OWE TO MY ANGEL MOTHER"

— ABRAHAM LINCOLN

You make the best...

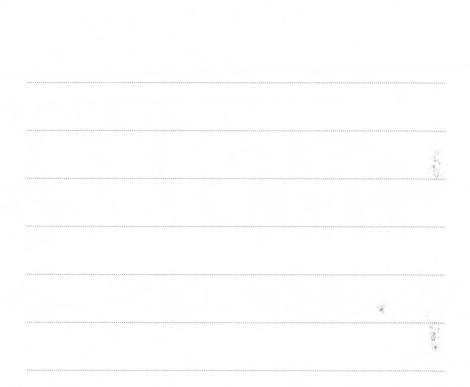

COLOR ME!

PASTE IN A PHOTO
OR
DRAW SOMETHING!

"ACCEPTANCE, TOLERANCE, BRAVERY, COMPASSION.
THESE ARE THE THINGS MY MOM TAUGHT ME."
—LADY GAGA

MOM

Nutrition Facts

Serving Size: 1 Awesome Woman

	% Daily Value*
Unconditional Love	1000%
Patience	800%
Unparalleled Skill	500%
Hard Work	100%
Self Sacrifice	100%
Multitasking	110% + 110%
Sleep	1%
Caffeine	150%
Wrong Answers	0%
Regret	0%

* Percent Daily Values may be higher or lower based on the behavior of the child

"LIFE BEGAN WITH WAKING UP
AND LOVING MY MOTHER'S FACE."
—GEORGE ELIOT

You make the best...

You have an amazing talent for...

"OVER THE YEARS,
I LEARNED SO MUCH FROM MOM.
SHE TAUGHT ME ABOUT THE IMPORTANCE OF
HOME AND HISTORY AND FAMILY AND TRADITION.
SHE ALSO TAUGHT ME THAT AGING NEED NOT MEAN
NARROWING THE SCOPE OF YOUR ACTIVITIES AND
INTERESTS OR A DIMINUTION OF THE GREAT PLEASURES
TO BE HAD IN THE EVERYDAY."

—MARTHA STEWART

SUPERLIST #3

Mom, here are just a few **words** to describe you:

[CHECK ALL THAT APPLY]

- ❑ fun
- ❑ caring
- ❑ kind
- ❑ loving
- ❑ thoughtful
- ❑ strong
- ❑ brave
- ❑ funny
- ❑ creative
- ❑ considerate
- ❑ beautiful

- ❑ independent
- ❑ awesome
- ❑ supportive
- ❑ tough
- ❑ brilliant
- ❑ smart
- ❑ generous
- ❑ cool
- ❑ hip
- ❑ bossy (ha!)
- ❑ humble

❑ _____

"MY MOTHER WAS THE MOST BEAUTIFUL WOMAN I EVER SAW.

ALL I AM I OWE TO MY MOTHER.

I ATTRIBUTE MY SUCCESS IN LIFE TO THE MORAL,

INTELLECTUAL AND PHYSICAL EDUCATION I RECEIVED FROM HER."

—GEORGE WASHINGTON

I love when we do these things together...

AMAZING
LOVING
STRONG
HAPPY
SELFLESS
GRACEFUL

YOU ARE ALL THOSE THINGS & MORE!

I wish I had more time to do these things with you...

"MOTHER IS A VERB.

IT'S SOMETHING YOU DO. NOT JUST WHO YOU ARE."
— DOROTHY CANFIELD FISHER

I love hearing stories about your...

"LOVE AS POWERFUL AS YOUR MOTHER'S FOR YOU
LEAVES ITS OWN MARK...
TO HAVE BEEN LOVED SO DEEPLY...
WILL GIVE US SOME PROTECTION FOREVER."
—J.K. ROWLING

I'm thankful I got your...

I love getting your advice on...

"MOTHER'S LOVE IS PEACE.
IT NEED NOT BE ACQUIRED,
IT NEED NOT BE DESERVED."
– ERICH FROMM

Some things I LOVE about
MOM

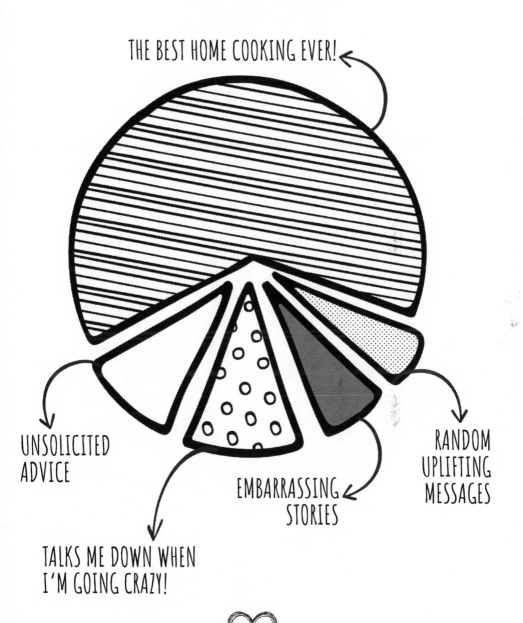

THE BEST HOME COOKING EVER!

UNSOLICITED
ADVICE

TALKS ME DOWN WHEN
I'M GOING CRAZY!

EMBARRASSING
STORIES

RANDOM
UPLIFTING
MESSAGES

"A MOTHER IS SHE WHO CAN TAKE THE PLACE OF ALL OTHERS
BUT WHOSE PLACE NO ONE ELSE CAN TAKE."
— CARDINAL MEYMILLOD

If you were a scent, you'd be...

FIND ALL THE
HEARTS

COLOR THEM!

PASTE IN A PHOTO
OR
DRAW SOMETHING!

"YOUR JOB AS A PARENT IS TO LISTEN.
AND TO DOLE OUT AS MUCH LOVE AS YOU CAN.
THAT INCLUDES TOUGH LOVE."
—CHRISTIE BRINKLEY

I love how good you are at...

THANK YOU FOR HELPING ME
RISE & BLOSSOM.

The best adventure we've had together was......

–MOTHERS–
PROTECTIVE & FIERCE

Thank you for being patient with me when...

"I BELIEVE THE CHOICE TO BECOME A MOTHER
IS THE CHOICE TO BECOME ONE OF THE GREATEST
SPIRITUAL TEACHERS THERE IS."
— OPRAH WINFREY

 **SUPERLIST #4**

Mom, if you were a **Famous TV Mom** you would be...

[CHECK ALL THAT APPLY]

☐ **Carol Brady**
The Brady Bunch
THE HIP MULTITASKING MOM
Understanding with great advice to any problem.

☐ **Claire Huxtable**
The Cosby Show
THE PROFESSIONAL MOM
Perfect balance of elegance and toughness. Book-smart & street-smart.

☐ **Marion Cunningham**
Happy Days
THE OLD FASHIONED MOM
Caretaker, loved by all. Happy to take in those in need.

☐ **Lucy Ricardo**
I Love Lucy
THE HILARIOUS MOM
Always has a new plan on how to get more likes on Instagram. Fun!

☐ **Samantha Stephens**
Bewitched
THE MAGICAL MOM
Diplomatic family peace maker. Some say she solves problems magically.

☐ **Marge Simpson**
The Simpsons
THE REALLY PATIENT MOM
Loving, thoughtful and just rolls her eyes at her family's hi-jinks.

☐ **Lorelai Gilmore**
The Gilmore Girls
THE COOL MOM.
Funny, down-to-earth and endlessly supportive. Your Friends love her.

☐ **Gloria Delgado-Pritchett**
Modern Family
THE HOT MOM
Sassy. Yells to get her family's attention. Young beyond her years.

☐ **Claire Dunphy**
Modern Family
THE BOSSY MOM
A tad uptight & controlling, but fiercely loyal and amusing.

☐ **Peggy Bundy**
Married with Children
THE REBEL MOM
Unapologetically rebukes the whole notion of doting housewife.

MOM,

YOU GAVE ME A WONDERFUL CHILDHOOD AND CONTINUE TO BRING JOY TO MY LIFE. THANK YOU SO MUCH.

I never get tired of your...

MOM

I LOVE YOU LOADS!

AND THANK YOU FOR DOING ALL OF THAT...

Laundry

When I was a kid, I thought the best thing about you was...

"IT'S NOT EASY BEING A MOTHER.
IF IT WERE, FATHERS WOULD DO IT."
—GOLDEN GIRLS

It makes me laugh to think how you...

MOMS ARE THE PEOPLE WHO KNOW US THE BEST
AND LOVE US THE MOST.

I have to admit you're always right about...

WISE COOL
PROTECTIVE MOM HERO
FANTASTIC
COMPASSIONATE SWEET
FUN BRAVE
LOVING AMAZING LOYAL
MUM
CARING
FAIR
KIND

I appreciate this most about you today...

"SOMETIMES I OPEN MY MOUTH...
AND MY MOTHER COMES OUT."

There are things we have been in agreement about...

....

....

....

....

....

....

HOME IS WHERE YOUR MOM IS.

 # SUPERLIST #5

Mom, if you were a **DRINK**
you would be...

[CHECK ALL THAT APPLY]

☐ **Coffee**
"Perky" - Full of Energy

☐ **Beer**
You're such a "Hoppy" person

☐ **Wine**
You deal with lots of whining

☐ **Margarita**
Salty & Sweet

☐ **Martini**
Straight Up & Strong

☐ **Tea**
You're all for hearing it or spilling it.

☐ **Aperol Spritz**
Pleasant & Bright + hint of tang

☐ **Champagne**
Bubbly & Effervescent

☐ **Cosmopolitan**
Sweet but watch out for the kick.

☐ **Water**
Earthy & Healthy

☐ _____

MOM, you're GREAT

COLOR ME!

PASTE IN A PHOTO
OR
DRAW SOMETHING!

"A MOTHER IS THE TRUEST FRIEND WE HAVE,
WHEN TRIALS HEAVY AND SUDDEN FALL UPON US;
WHEN ADVERSITY TAKES THE PLACE OF PROSPERITY;
WHEN FRIENDS DESERT US;
WHEN TROUBLE THICKENS AROUND US,
STILL WILL SHE CLING TO US,
AND ENDEAVOR BY HER KIND PRECEPTS AND
COUNSELS TO DISSIPATE THE CLOUDS OF DARKNESS,
AND CAUSE PEACE TO RETURN TO OUR HEARTS."
—WASHINGTON IRVING

There are also things we have disagreed about...

I THINK YOU'RE DANDY...
AND I'M NOT LION.

I think it's awesome that you...

MOM...

I DONUT

KNOW WHAT I WOULD DO WITHOUT YOU!

My favorite food that you make for me is...

MOTHERS HOLD THEIR CHILDREN'S HANDS FOR A SHORT WHILE,
BUT THEIR HEARTS FOREVER.

I would love to go here with you...

EVERYTHING I AM
YOU HELPED ME TO BE

You are there for me when...

MOM

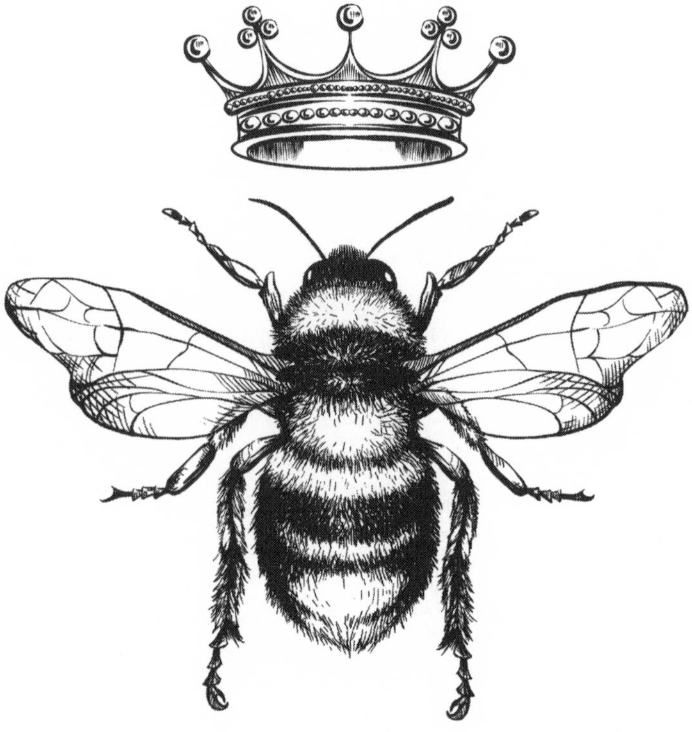

the title above

QUEEN

MOM

[mäm] *noun*

1. someone who sees the best in her kids even when they drive her crazy.

2. unconditional love

3. someone who does the work of twenty for free.

See also: superwoman, saint

"GOD COULD NOT BE EVERYWHERE,
AND THEREFORE HE MADE MOTHERS."
—RUDYARD KIPLING

I love it when you call me...

A MOM'S HUG LASTS LONG AFTER SHE LETS GO.

Mom, if you were a **Song** you would be...
[CHECK ALL THAT APPLY]

☐ **R-E-S-P-E-C-T** *(Aretha Franklin)*
Because you demand it and deserve it!

☐ **My Way** *(Frank Sinatra)*
Because you taught me to do things this way...

☐ **If It Makes You Happy** *(Sheryl Crow)*
Because you told me to do things for this reason

☐ **I Will Survive** *(Gloria Gaynor)*
Your anthem while raising me

☐ **That Don't Impress Me Much** *(Shania Twain)*
What you said when I did something dumb

☐ **Girls Just Want To Have Fun** *(Cyndi Lauper)*
When you had a well deserved night off

☐ **I Will Always Love You** *(Whitney Houston)*
Because I do and I will.

☐ _____

YOU'RE A KOALA-TY MOM!

When I was little, I loved to watch you...

"IT MAY BE POSSIBLE TO GILD PURE GOLD,
BUT WHO CAN MAKE HIS MOTHER MORE BEAUTIFUL?"
—MAHATMA GANDHI

Sometimes your ability to do this amazes me....

FLOWERS LOOK UP AT THE SUN
CHILDREN LOOK UP TO THEIR MOTHERS

I love your taste in...

COLOR ME!

THANKS FOR OWL YOU DO!

PASTE IN A PHOTO
OR
DRAW SOMETHING!

"MOTHERS NEVER RETIRE,
NO MATTER HOW OLD HER CHILDREN ARE
SHE IS ALWAYS A MOM,
ALWAYS WILLING TO ENCOURAGE AND
HELP HER CHILDREN IN ANY WAY SHE CAN!"
—CATHERINE PULSIFER

I always want to hear what you're going to say about...

I'M PROUD TO BE Y'ORCHID

One of the most fun things we've done together was...

MOM

YOU'RE A REAL

GEM

Sorry for all the times I've said
and done something stupid,
like when...

"TO DESCRIBE MY MOTHER
WOULD BE TO WRITE ABOUT A HURRICANE IN ITS PERFECT POWER."
—MAYA ANGELOU

A special memory
I have of you is...

THANK YOU

MOM

FOR EVERYTHING

Thank you for...

....

....

....

....

....

....

I Love You!

If you love this book...
would you please leave us a review?

Made in the USA
Middletown, DE
19 June 2022

67395752R00066